happiness is...

happiness is...

LISA MESSENGER

Messenger Publishing

First published in 2004

Messenger Publishing
PO Box H241
Australia Square NSW 1215
Email: info@happinessis.com.au
www.happinessis.com.au

Copyright © Lisa Messenger

All rights reserved. No part of this book may be reproduced or transmitted in any form or by any means, electronic or mechanical, including photocopying, recording or by any information storage and retrieval system, without prior permission in writing from the publisher. The Australian Copyright Act 1968 (the Act) allows a maximum of one chapter or 10 per cent of this book, whichever is the greater, to be photocopied by any educational institution for its educational purposes provided that the educational institution (or body that administers it) has given a remuneration notice to Copyright Agency Limited (CAL) under the Act.

National Library of Australia Cataloguing-in-Publication data:

Messenger, Lisa.
   Happiness is -.
   ISBN 0 646 43573 6.
     1. Happiness - Popular works. 2. Australians - Pictorial works. I. Title.

152.43

Concept by Lisa Messenger
Art direction and design by Russell Jeffery, emigraph
Additional art direction by Lisa Messenger
Legal counsel: Abbott Tout

Where multiple images appear on one page, all images are by the same photographer (except where indicated).
All words provided by subjects or photographers are their own and do not express the views of the publisher.
All images supplied by photographers or subjects have been credited to the photographer as acknowledged when received. The publisher takes no responsibility for ensuring these details have been supplied correctly.
All attempts were made to locate any photographers not credited in this book
All photographs have been put into sections for structure. We recognise that many of the photographs would fit across many sections.

Photos on pages vi, xi and xiii, © Katrina Hawley

Produced in China through Bookbuilders

To my grandfather who always believes in me,
and to children everywhere — may they achieve
true happiness ...

When one door of happiness closes,
another opens; but often we look so long
at the closed door that we do not see
the one which has been opened for us.

Helen Keller

viii kids help line

x introduction

CONTENTS

1 hope

20 joy

38 love

60 companions

80 innocence

112 freedom

140 passion

164 spirtuality

184 towns

186 photographic credits

192 acknowledgements

Kids Help Line Marketing Team...

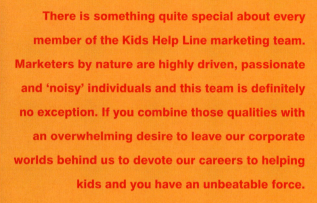

There is something quite special about every member of the Kids Help Line marketing team. Marketers by nature are highly driven, passionate and 'noisy' individuals and this team is definitely no exception. If you combine those qualities with an overwhelming desire to leave our corporate worlds behind us to devote our careers to helping kids and you have an unbeatable force.

There is no reward like the one we receive at the end of every project knowing that the money we have raised will help answer a call from a young person in need. Family relationships, bullying, eating disorders, grief, loneliness and suicide. Every day we help, in our own little way, to address these and many other cries for help from Australian kids.

We're always creating new and exciting ways for people and companies to connect with Kids Help Line. Some of our successful initiatives include: Lock Up Your Boss Day, Business Chicks Breakfasts, BisiNetwork and the Give Kids A Voice Weekend.

Carmel Molloy
National Marketing Director Kids Help Line
Phone: (02) 9415 4011 / Email: khnsw@kidshelp.com.au
www.kidshelp.com.au

INTRODUCTION

This book is my long overdue indulgence — a book about the best thing in life — happiness and its pursuit.

I've always been quite a passionate, driven person — always striving for more, changing the rules as I go and taking a non traditional approach to pretty much everything in life. I've loved my journey. I've lived in some amazing places, had some bizarre and adventurous experiences and have had some incredible jobs.

For years I've committed myself to managing other people's dreams and passions and even though I've had huge amounts of freedom the past three years with my own company, it was time for another creative outlet.

Events in my life led me to the decision to create something of my own that made me happy and would enable me to come up with my own creative ways of sharing that happiness. I wanted something which would encompass and involve people from all over Australia on a number of levels — either being part of its development, being showcased, or being able to buy it and enjoy it.

Research showed that there were a number of beautiful photographic books in the market and many truly inspirational books as well. But there was little I could find that combined the two with a pure Australian focus.

I called on photographers from all over Australia and have to thank all the professionals and the emerging photographers from the various schools and colleges, for making my vision come to life. The response was overwhelming.

It has been a fast and euphoric ride — a real six month natural high. From the start I visualised every aspect of the book from concept, design, distribution, alliances, marketing, right down to the chapter breakdowns and fonts. With the help of my brilliant designer, Russell Jeffery, it became a reality.

Putting the book together has been one of the happiest times of my life. I hope that you find this book exciting and stimulating both visually and verbally and that it brings you joy.

happiness is...

I am absolutely thrilled to give a portion of the proceeds to Kids Help Line. Kids Help Line provides an invaluable service to the kids of Australia. It is the only 24-hour confidential and anonymous telephone and online counselling service for kids aged 5–18. Each week counsellors respond to over 10,000 calls from kids in need. Thousands more continue to go unanswered. More financial assistance is needed desperately.

The proceeds from the sales of this book will help fund more services and make our children, families and communities stronger and indeed happier.

Lisa Messenger

I believe happiness is essential to our fulfilment as a human being. Volker Krohn, a close friend, a source of inspiration, awareness and change for me kindly wrote these words recently: —

The comparing mind is always at risk. Happiness is never really experienced when it is conditional on achieving something other than what one has or is. Being at peace with ourselves and with others moves us beyond conditional happiness to another level.

The power of love, trite as it might sound, seems to be the basis of the human experience of happiness. Finding compassion, forgiveness and love for the people who have injured us in the past, including ourselves, is the most effective way to achieve contentment and happiness in one's life.

I hope this book will inspire you, the reader, as it did myself, to find the courage to express what "turns you on", what gets the "mojo" rising, what makes you happy. Even if we are pursuing conditional happiness, just the expression of what gives us joy is already a step toward healing. Allow yourself to be seen in your joy. It's infectious and inspires others.

Volker Krohn, Director Hoffman Centre, Australia and Singapore
The Hoffman Quadrinity Process – An eight day profoundly emotional rollercoaster ride a la Freud meets Walt Disney www.quadrinity.com.au

HOPE

A tree bravely growing on a cliff face. That's hope.

To me, hope is more subtle than emotions such as love, passion or joy. But don't underestimate the power of hope. Hope gives us optimism; it frees us from pessimism and from submission and allows us to believe that anything is possible.

Hope, with passion and commitment can deliver our dreams.

Despite world atrocities and setbacks, everyday we witness incredible stories of survival against all kinds of adversity and this provides hope. People choose to make positive changes, uphold their values and live in unity. They retain a strong sense of family and community built on acceptance and co-operation. Perhaps these people have a deeper understanding of a universal consciousness that unites us all.

There is a life force in hope. It makes me think of inner strength and a will to live. People with hope are positive and willing to go beyond limitations and boundaries. Hope gives happiness a chance. Hope opens the door and lets happiness in.

Hope with grace and humility — that's an unbeatable combination.

Lisa

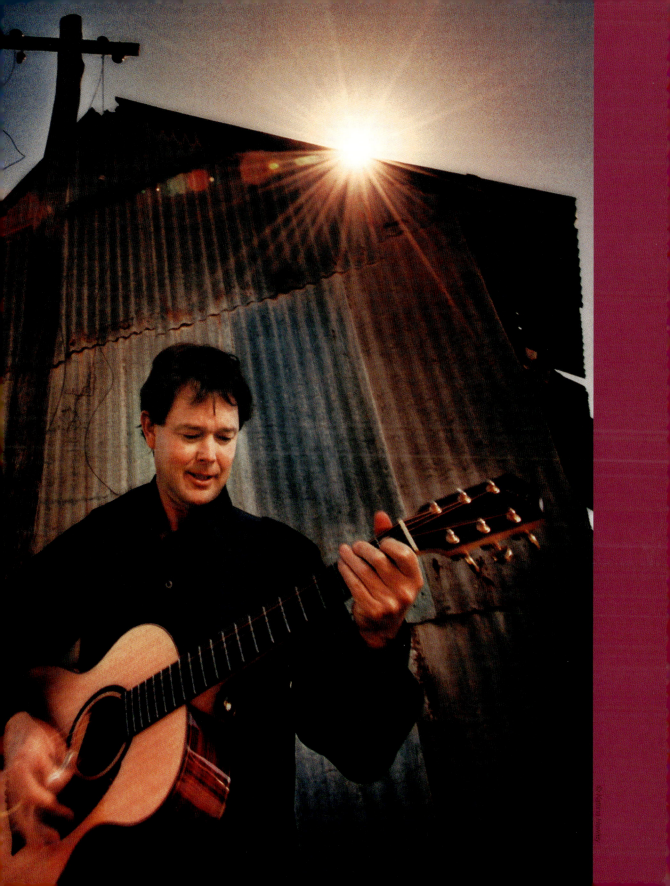

My son arrived by emergency caesarean, more than six weeks before his due date. Screened from the action, I did not see his birth. My first contact was when my tiny baby was briefly placed near my head on the operating table. After less than a minute, Thomas was taken away to be examined by doctors.

The lungs are one of the last organs to mature before birth, however the fact that Thomas had drawn breath and cried was a fantastic indication that his very premature lungs were working. He was well enough for me to touch him again briefly before he was taken to a special care nursery.

But further investigation showed he was severely anaemic, depriving him of oxygen. A blood transfusion was ordered and a transfer to the city's only neonatal intensive care unit arranged. Before this could be done, Thomas' condition worsened and he stopped breathing. Following his ordeal before and during his birth, his tiny body was simply too tired to keep his lungs and heart working. He was resuscitated and transferred by ambulance to the ICU.

A few hours later, I was also transferred by ambulance so I could be close to Thomas.
Now the extent of his illness became clear. On top of the anaemia, he was suffering from severe respiratory distress, unable to breathe on his own. He was covered in tubes and wires, and heavily sedated. Still on a hospital trolley after the caesarean, I was taken into the ICU and was able to touch Thomas for the first time since his birth. Even this small contact gave me hope – especially when Thomas opened his eyes and looked directly at me. From that point, I was never convinced that he was the 'very sick' baby everyone described him as.

For the next several days, Thomas' life was measured in hours, and every small change in his condition was significant. During this time, Thomas received three transfusions and was moved onto a different ventilator. Once his condition stabilised and he started to improve, progress was dramatic and surprising. Finally he was able to be lifted off his special bed and be held for the first time by his mother. This skin-to-skin contact alleviated all the physical and mental pain of recent days. I was convinced now that his full recovery was only a matter of time.

Within a week, he was breathing on his own, and was ready to be moved out of ICU. Thomas' second ride in an ambulance was a much happier affair – being transferred back to the hospital where he was born, which is close to the home we hoped to take him to soon. Again, progress was rapid, and mother and baby spent much time together making up for lost days. It was not long before the last of the tubes and monitors were removed, and he was feeding well enough to go home.

We joke that Thomas has inherited his father's optimism and his mother's stubbornness — this may well be true, and stood him in good stead as he overcame every difficulty thrown at him in his first days. What is happiness? Happiness is looking into the eyes of my son and hearing him cry with all the strength of his healed lungs.

happiness is...

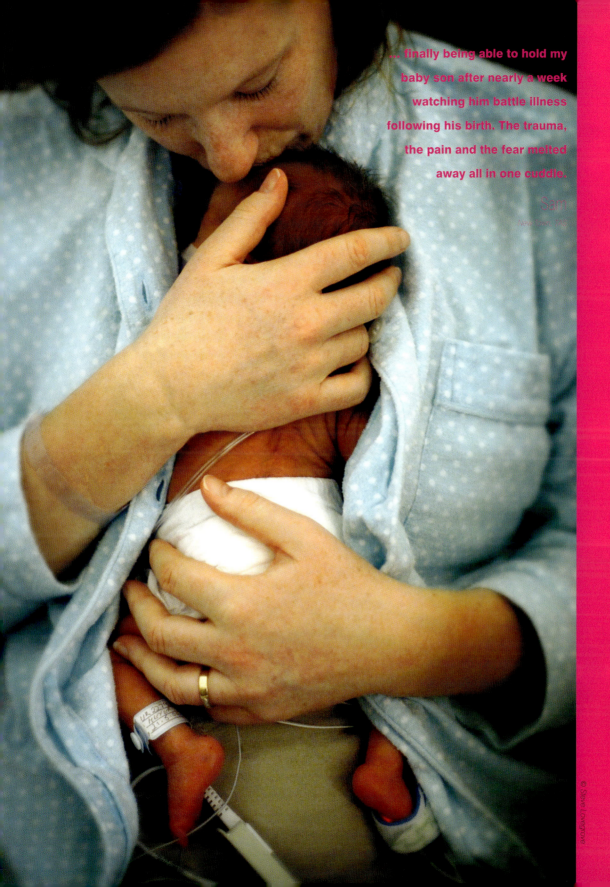

... finally being able to hold my baby son after nearly a week watching him battle illness following his birth. The trauma, the pain and the fear melted away all in one cuddle.

Sam

...hope

Just Hold On

When the night closes in around you
And you feel that no one really cares
When you hope that someone somewhere hears you
And you feel that this might be the end

Chorus

Just hold on
Cause there's someone who cares
Just reach out and take hold of my hand
Just stand still and hear my voice inside you
Just hold on cause I am here with you

When the days seem to lose all purpose
And the people rush and pass you by
When your life seems to lose all meaning
And your heart gives up all its fight

Chorus

Bridge

You don't have to worry
You don't have to fear
Just put your trust in me today
And I always will be here

...hope

... getting inspiration from my quiet time with God to then join a melody with lyrics that can touch peoples lives.

Arrnott
Bondi, NSW

happiness is...

... discovering wild places and wild creatures. Nothing inspires or delights me more than the natural wonders of this world. I cannot go back in time to see what was but I can go to the edge of the world to see what is. I believe balance is a myth, so I will climb any mountain, brave any desert and cross any ocean if it means connecting with the astonishing and beautiful creatures who share our planet. I have it on good authority that the priceless elixir of eternal youth can be created naturally simply by staring into the eyes of a curious Uakari or inhaling the breath of a Tasmanian forest. After such an experience you may stop smiling when you are asleep, though I can't be certain.

Bradley
Chain of Lagoons, TAS

...hope

happiness is…

… making your dreams come true. Being at one with yourself and the world around you. Doing the impossible. Overcoming your fears. Wearing a smile. Sharing vegetarian sushi with friends. Loving your family. A hot sunny day at the beach. Bright coloured flowers. Dancing the night away. Never giving up. Not making excuses and having no regrets. Happiness is life's greatest gift because you can give it to yourself!

Marayke
Maroochydore, QLD

...hope

sharing

happiness is...

... spending time with my wife and son. After twelve years of marriage, our baby son is the great joy of our life.

John
Bilgola, NSW

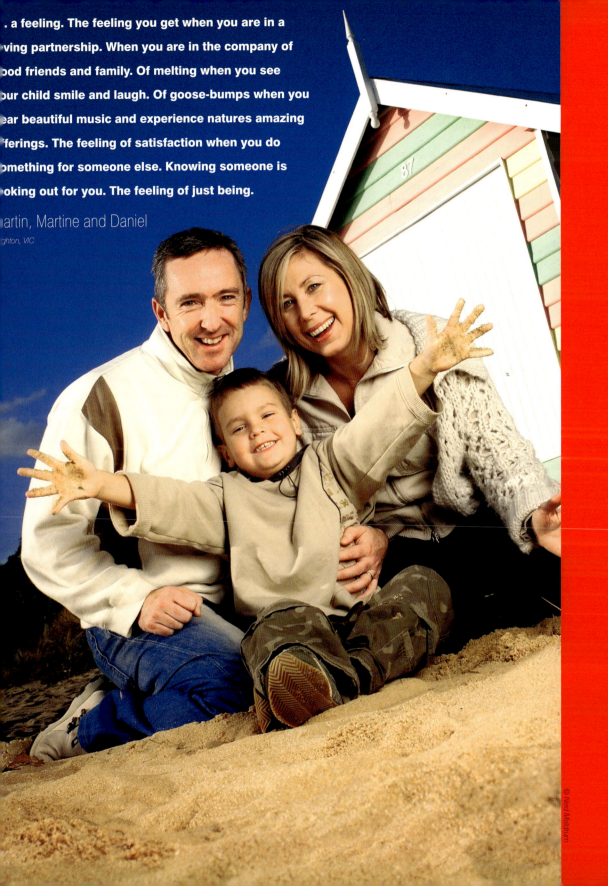

... a feeling. The feeling you get when you are in a loving partnership. When you are in the company of good friends and family. Of melting when you see your child smile and laugh. Of goose-bumps when you hear beautiful music and experience natures amazing offerings. The feeling of satisfaction when you do something for someone else. Knowing someone is looking out for you. The feeling of just being.

Martin, Martine and Daniel
Brighton, VIC

...hope

© Ned Meldrum

... to share life with your grandchildren is indeed happiness.

Robert
Kialla, VIC

... hope

experience

happiness is....

... leaving all expectation behind and living in this very moment. Tasting the aroma of life and awakening to the beauty of the world.

Byron
Paddington, QLD

... watching kids having a terrific time. Their shrieks of laughter filled the night air. They were so absorbed in laughter, completely oblivious that it was getting dark and no one else was in the water.

Cathy
Macleod Park, VIC

...hope

creativity

happiness is…

… spending your days doing something you love and believe in wholeheartedly.

Kate
Bellevue Hill, NSW

... **watching and helping my children in any way I can to reach their full potential in the course of their lives. In turn, their happiness is reflected back to me in rewards such as unconditional love, trust and respect. The bus represents one time spent together to solidify our bonds as a family.**

Jane
Berry, NSW

...hope

happiness is...

... my family, my health and my happiness (and the happiness of those about whom I care).

Tim
Sydney, NSW

© Richard Miller

18

... **spending time with my family. Here my daughter Lily Kate and I are laughing at our bellies three weeks before our new baby is due to arrive.**

Sally
Leederville, WA

Joy

For me, joy is an overwhelming wave of complete and utter happiness. It is that feeling of inner radiance when you are literally beaming from the inside out.

There is something celebratory about joy. It's more than just being happy. It's being exultant. Because it's a celebration it almost always involves something or someone other than myself. When we share significant events and delight in another person's happiness we experience the wonder of really connecting with others.

Why are we afraid of too much joy? Why do we defer this happiness? We often let negativity or neuroses dictate what we feel and do, leaving us anxious and unfulfilled.

Don't keep putting things off — postponing happiness. Be happy where you are right now, otherwise you'll always be living for the future. Consciously try to live for the moment. When I live in the moment, I am consumed wholeheartedly by joy.

Now I live in the present and enjoy all its moments.

Lisa

... living each day in anticipation. Living each moment without regret. Living life with the ones you love.

Hai
Queens Park, WA

happiness is …

shopping

... dancing round the house in my favourite pair of shoes.

Claire
Darlinghurst, NSW

... **the warmth of my daughter in my arms as she tells stories in her innocent baby way.**

Chris
Leederville, WA

happiness is...

... just me and my Dad, laughing and laughing and laughing.

Amelia

Tocumwal, NSW

...joy

happiness is...

... being able to wear
my hair naturally

... gazing adoringly into
the mirror and seeing
how truly fabulous I am

... being able to wear
REAL FAKE FUR

... when you're lucky enough
to be one of my best girlfriends

... cosmetics abuse

... Botox, Detox, and Paralox

... WHATEVER!

Miss Pencil Vania
Whitfield Heights, QLD

...joy

happiness is…

…having a loving family, good friends to rely on and a contented lifestyle.

Jon
Quindalup, WA

... the freedom to explore and experience the beauty and wonder of nature.

happiness is... Nadene, Centennial Park, NSW

... knowing that you are free to be who you want, say what you feel and go where you please. To be free is to be truly happy.

Roza
Edgecliff, NSW

happiness is...

...a romantic stroll through a pine forest on our wedding day!

Jane and Brendan
Hampton, VIC

happiness is…

… finding your soulmate and every subsequent second spent together.

Saul
currently living in London, UK

happiness is…

… a way of being. To be happy means that you can find the joy, love and laughter in life and live within those feelings. To me, finding my true passion in life has enabled me to find my happiness. I now surround myself with flowers, essential oils and people and inspire others to be happy – and I call this WORK! This is not work. It is a way of life that I have chosen that makes me happy.

Briohney
Castle Cove, NSW

LOVE

Why does it take a long time to realise where love begins? It begins, of course, inside all of us and some learn that sooner than others. Self love and love of life is one of the keys to happiness.

Love comes in many forms — not always romantic love. Love is all around us. It's a child's smile, a thoughtful gesture to a lonely neighbour, a heartfelt thank you. Love unconditionally, expect nothing in return and magically, love will deliver the serendipity of finding blessings we didn't look for or expect. Love is pure and beautiful. Real love has no conditions attached.

Take responsibility for your own actions and allow others just to be. Rather than hold onto resentment, reach out, apologise and let others be right. The inner satisfaction will be well worth it — knowing that your actions, even in a small way, make the world a more peaceful, loving place.

Receiving love from others is something you can't control. Concentrate on giving more love and you will receive more. Love given freely is the only love that can satisfy. You can't barter or trade love. Give it generously and unconditionally; it is sure to return.

Lisa

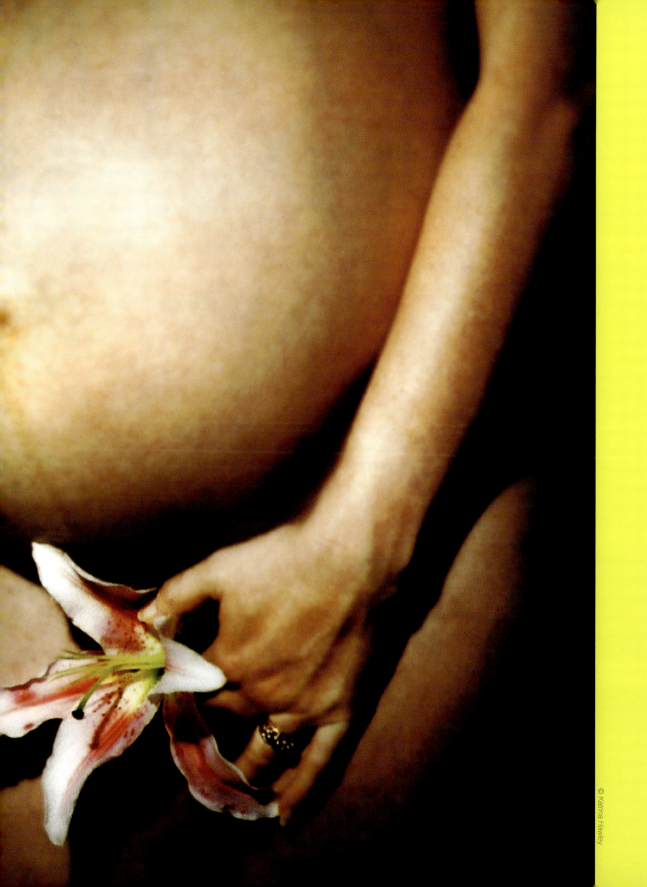

© Karina Hawley

... when I hold Cody and he looks at me with those eyes full of trust and unconditional love, my heart swells with emotion.

John

happiness is...

… living in a healthy, happy, Christian family and appreciating all the wonderful relationships and phenomena of the natural world.

Hannah
Gordon, NSW

happiness is…

... Sunday

In the chaos of my life, Sunday offers everything I cherish wrapped into 24 hours. It's the only day of week my family is always together. The grin on my son's face when he wakes up says exactly what we're all thinking: you're both here, all mine, all day. Some Sundays we spend at home, just hanging around doing very little but enjoying each other's company. Other Sundays are filled with adventure or in the company of our favourite people. But wherever we are and whatever we do, my Sundays are all about laughing and smiling until my cheeks hurt and falling in love over and over again with my beautiful boys.

Donna
Paddington, NSW

happiness is…

… my first mothers day with my beautiful baby boy. Just sitting there with my husband and talking to each other as we had our first bath together.

Rose
Cecil Hills, NSW

...love

... doing fun and exciting things with the family.

Amy, Caitlin and Jared
Burwood, NSW

happiness is...

... the laughter of friends and the security of a supportive environment.

Rae
Opossum Bay, VIC

... the precious time spent with family all together.

Olivia
Dunsborough, WA

...love

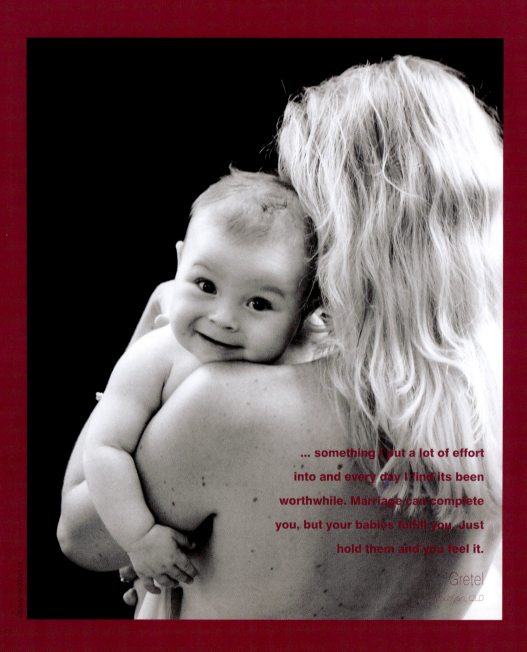

happiness is…

… something I put a lot of effort into and every day I find its been worthwhile. Marriage can complete you, but your babies fulfill you. Just hold them and you feel it.

Gretel
Msunjan, QLD

... for me those moments in life in between running a business, being a mum, wife, friend, rushing around like a mad woman, when you suddenly stop and think — life is good.
I do enjoy this.
It can be when I'm pushing the pram on our morning walk, or stepping out onto a city street after a great meeting, opening the front door on a beautiful sunny day, or hearing the *glug glug* of wine pouring into the glass.

Stephanie
Leichhardt, NSW

...love

happiness is…

dreams

… smiling at someone and seeing them smile back.

Larry
North Perth, WA

...love

happiness is....

... the simple things in life. Wheather it be the smiles from my two children in the morning, a hug that comes from nowhere or just uncontrolled laughter.

Jason
Mosman, NSW

... knowing that all the hard work you put in at the beginning is well worth it in the end. You are holding their tiny hands and cradling their bodies, then it seems a minute later they are holding your hands, cuddling you.

Debbie
Paddington, NSW

happiness is…

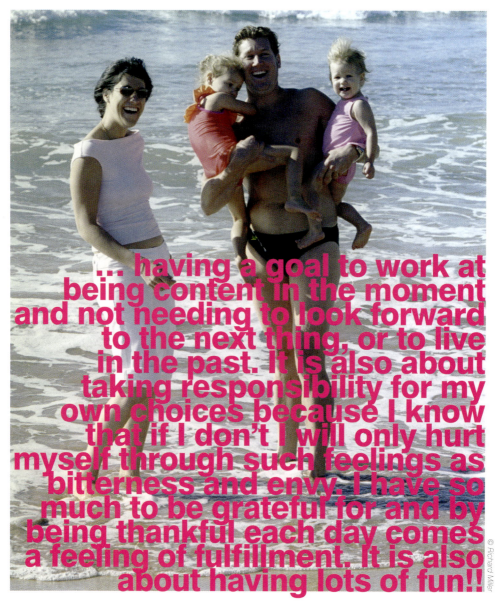

… having a goal to work at being content in the moment and not needing to look forward to the next thing, or to live in the past. It is also about taking responsibility for my own choices because I know that if I don't I will only hurt myself through such feelings as bitterness and envy. I have so much to be grateful for and by being thankful each day comes a feeling of fulfillment. It is also about having lots of fun!!

Nicole
Roseville, NSW

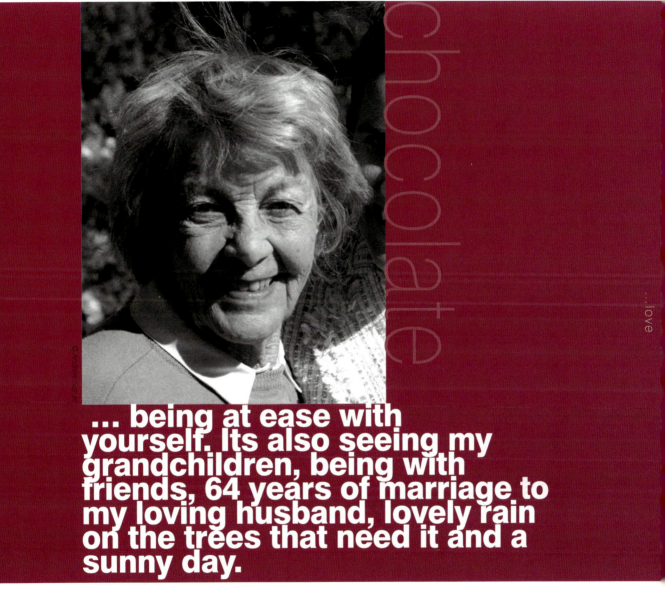

chocolate ...love

… being at ease with yourself. Its also seeing my grandchildren, being with friends, 64 years of marriage to my loving husband, lovely rain on the trees that need it and a sunny day.

Tottie
Woollahra, NSW

happiness is…

… spending time with my family. Having Nicholas has been the most rewarding thing I have ever done in my life. When I see my husband and son interact I develop an overwhelming feeling of happiness.

Melinda
Collaroy, NSW

… about feeling good within yourself and enjoying life. Happiness can make a difference in your life and those around you. Happiness is an 'abstract' noun that cannot be described in few words.

Christina
Como West, NSW

…love

... comes in moments and they are different from day to day. On this day, our friend Jim made us stand in the cold and rain for more than an hour while he took photographs of us. Fortunately he tells good jokes as he works.

Anni and Andrew
Robertson, NSW

© Jim Rolon

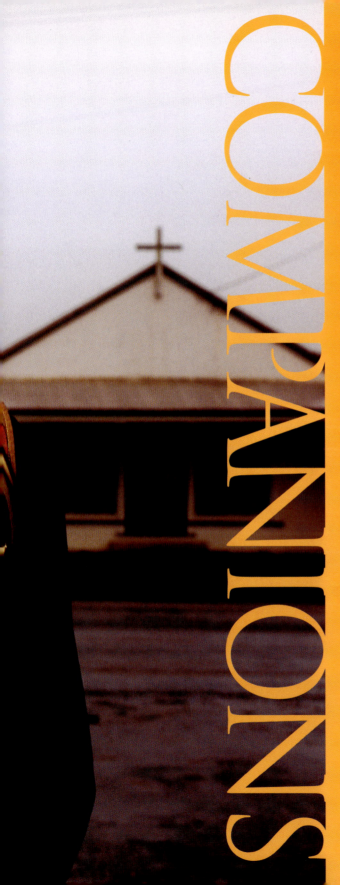

COMPANIONS

To sit beside another in comfortable silence.
To allow another to see into our heart and know our deepest thoughts.
To share dreams, hopes and fears.

Comfort and care.
An invisible bond.
Confidence that the other will know and understand.
A connection that cannot be severed.

When I think of companionship I think of all these things. I also think of my two beautiful Burmese cats, Reggie and Poppet, and how much I value their companionship.

The joys and blessings of companionship deepen over time. I think of an old couple, each supporting the other, hands held with an intimacy shaped by trust, time and shared memories.

My grandparents — loving and in love after 64 years.

Lisa

happiness is…

… anywhere my husband and our (totally pampered) pooches are!

Mayjan
Prahran, VIC

... getting together with my immediate family and my relatives.

Elizabeth
Armidale, NSW

... being alive.

Peter
Armidale, NSW

happiness is….

... the sights, sounds and smells of Sydney in summer and relaxing with the people (and pets) closest to me. Happiness to my dog (Toby) is two simple words — 'walk' and 'dinner'.

Katrina
Rozelle, NSW

happiness is… creamé sherry

… making other people happy. Doing the best I can at whatever I do.

Jean
Lake Munmorah, NSW

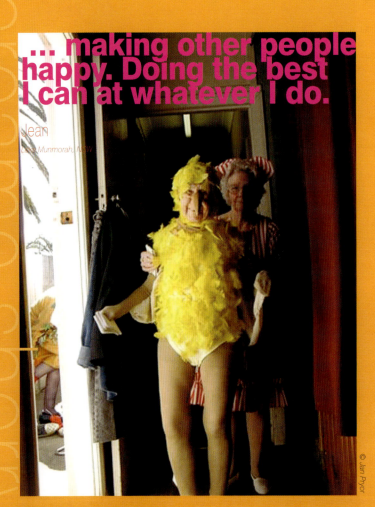
© Jan Pryor

Grandma is 92… and still performs in plays. She was a 'bird' in this case. She inspires everyone who meets her. At 92 she still goes out every Saturday night – loves to sing, dance, laugh, cook and has so many words of wisdom.

... precious moments with the 'little man'.

Russell
Cammeray, NSW

... love, family, friends, my dogs and bicycle and being lucky enough to have and enjoy these things. Happiness is the only real thing I strive for in life!

Jessica

Newtown, NSW

happiness is…

... spending time with my wife, my dog and my family. Coming back from a spinal injury — they were all there for me.

Ben
Zetland, NSW

... in my life
Because music has woven a path through me
Through many doors and places unseen
Love is the key
When I've stumbled and fallen
Come apart at the seams
It is my love for music thats healed
Because love is the key
Happiness – what a word.
For someone like you and me.
For it to grow, give and receive love
Because your love is the key
At the top of the mountain
Above all the world
You'll find happiness if you look there
Your love is your key

Paul
Mandurah, WA

happiness is…

… a warm, energising feeling that makes you smile, laugh and feel wonderful within yourself. It is a state of mind that can be chosen. To choose to feel happy is a good thing to achieve in life.

Janette and Tass
Aspendale Gardens, VIC

© Ian Clarke

... a life worth living; the reward of giving; the joy of sharing; the generosity of time; the comfort of good health; the closeness of family; being under the watchful eye of God.

Fay
Jindera, NSW

...companions

happiness is ...

... waking up in the morning and looking forward to the day ahead.

Vikki
Elanora Heights, NSW

... a fulfilling job, good friends, laughs, music, opportunity to travel and looking forward to good times ahead.

Brett
Mosman, NSW

... having a job where I am able to work with many different and amazing animals. Trying to make a difference and contributing to conservation.

Lindsay
Petersham, NSW

... self-acceptance

Ben
Rouse Hill, NSW

... a feeling of well-being, satisfaction and love. My happiest times are with people from all walks of life and going on all types of journeys.

Sam
Crows Nest, NSW

... the feeling of contentment that results from good experiences and/or good friends.

Ian
Herbord, NSW

... companions

happiness is...

... being married for 60 years. You have your ups and downs but still love one another and know what the other is thinking — that I think is happiness.

Pat and Arnold
Armidale, NSW

... believing in yourself and knowing anything is possible!

Cheeky Star

Bexley, NSW

INNOCENCE

That original state of unconscious knowing that all needs will be met and that love will be present and forthcoming.

The time before one learnt to be wary, defensive, worried, anxious, self conscious or fearful — before the experiences of punishment, practical jokes, taunts and rejection.

The time before understanding that others can hurt.

The time of being in the present moment, of wonder, certainty of self, delight in exploring and pushing the boundaries of the world further and further, of triumph in achievements.

Innocence embodied by a child's full trust and acceptance, their heartbreaking love, their shocking wisdom and forgiveness.

The fragility of innocence — and the ease with which words, looks and actions can take it away.

The glorious state to which we aspire — peace of mind, absolute contentment — the place we go in our dreams sometimes, the circle we complete at the end.

Wendy Reid, *Kids Help Line*

happiness is…

… eating lots of lollies, frog puppets, presents, birthday parties, dressing up.

Ellen
Iluka, WA

happiness is…

…feeling loved under my grandma's brolly.

Stephanie
Toorak, VIC

... being free.

...innocence

... I was glad I chose to do the pics of Oliver on the beach. As soon as he hit the sand he became a little crab, scurrying off in every direction... high-tailing it down to the water with his beautiful curls dancing in the wind. We got him near the boat and his Mum and Dad threw some toys inside so he would try and climb up to get them. This way we knew he would be entertained for at least a few seconds so I could snap this picture off. He's actually collapsing after using all his strength to peer over the top of the boat looking for his toys! He's a very happy, gorgeous, little terror and I found his two little bottom teeth so cheeky and irresistible. There was no problem getting him to smile, put it that way!

Katrina

# ... going out in Granddad's boat.

Brendan
Woodvale, WA

When asked if he enjoyed having his photo taken he replied 'Yes thank you, and Winky did too'.

happiness is….

… having a baby brother to play with!

Bec
Toorak, VIC

happiness is...

... warm sunny days, out to sea with my family and friends. Relaxed lifestyle of Noosa. Gentle rocking of the boat.

Joel
Cooroy, QLD

...innocence

happiness is…

... exploring new places, running, crawling and hiding in tall grass. Climbing trees and playing hide and seek.

Isabella
City Beach, WA

happiness is...

being young enough to think th[at]
everything makes me happ[y.]
Smiling and seeing smili[ng]
faces looking back at m[e.]

Ryle[y]
Bundaberg, Q[LD]

people

...innocence

... love without conditions.
Cuddles from your children.
Looking into their happy, smiling eyes.

Sandii
Kardinya, WA

happiness is…

© Kylee Priddle

… eating yummy food, camping with mummy and daddy and listening to my CD player.

Natalie
Coolum Beach, QLD

MRE!

Ayden
Cammeray, NSW

happiness is…

... **talking on the phone to my daddy when he is away at work.**

Cyrus
Twin Waters, QLD

...playing at the park, eating chocolate, playing dress-ups, playing with my friends.

Ruby
Beaconsfield, WA

...innocence

happiness is…

sport
family
friends
travelling
adventure

… when you have fun and laugh a lot.

Olivia
Robertson, NSW

...innocence

happiness is…

… doing things I've never done before like going to the beach because I live a long way from the ocean.

Lleyton
West Pingelly, WA

...innocence

... going out bush with family, playing on the beach and having fun.

Bianca

Maningrida, Arnhem Land

**... the miracle that I am.
Mum was told at the age of 15
she could never have a child.
We proved them wrong!**

Wally on behalf of Ayden
Matraville, NSW

...innocence

... playing with Lily at the beach and cuddling with her next to me at night.

being loved

...hearing my son really giggle. I can't help but laugh every time I hear it. It fills me with pure, physical joy.

Jodie
Quindalup, WA

happiness is...

... my friend Grace and I'm about to kiss her.

Lleyton
West Pingelly, WA

... warm, bright colours. Feeling as light as air.

Henry
Nedlands, WA

happiness is…

… learning, practicing and being proud of our culture.

Fonzy
Maningrida, Arnhem Land

Freedom is a release from something which would otherwise constrain us. Being free of fear is energising; being free of dependence makes us powerful.

Being free to express ourselves physically is not only liberating, it's another key to happiness. Research suggests that happy people are more active than unhappy people. In particular, happy people tend to spend more time engaging in activities that provide pleasure and satisfaction. Further, if you're not happy and you engage in activities that you usually find enjoyable then there's a good chance that your mood will soon improve.

Activity can free us in a number of ways. Exercise can contribute to a range of health benefits that are distinctly associated with positive moods. Being healthy makes it easier to for us to be free of illness and pain.

In addition, happy people tend to be more productive and more successful. Productivity and success in turn are often influential on mood and not surprisingly, tend to be associated more with positive mood states such as happiness.

To be happy, therefore, be busy. Specifically, make sure you engage in as many satisfying and enjoyable activities as possible. It's fine to relax but if you want pure relaxation, practice meditation or go for a nice walk. Don't expect to experience high levels of satisfaction or real happiness from 'veging' out in front of the TV!

Dr Timothy Sharp, The Happiness Institute
www.thehappinessinstitute.com.au

happiness is…

… being there. Being useful. Happiness is friends and family. Listening to mentally active and dedicated people. Happiness is space and quietitude. The birds singing, the frogs croaking. Looking beyond the hill. Being warm in winter.

Jean
Maida Vale, WA

distant horizons
...freedom

happiness is…

… seeing the unspoilt smiles on my children's faces and feeling the wind in my face riding a motorbike on the open road.

Craig
Five Dock, NSW

…participating in making others happy, seeing the elderly smile, playing with puppies, planning my next holiday, looking back on my life so far and being proud of who I am.

Janet
Five Dock, NSW

… a choice — a state of mind. Being married for 15 years to my wonderful husband, traveling and exploring new destinations, riding my Harley, laughing with girlfriends, family Christmas, my cat's purr, elderly people holding hands, discovering the perfect shoes on sale, a child's giggle, gifts from Tiffany & Co.

Neen
Artarmon, NSW

…freedom

... **a passion that gets into your blood and never goes away. The rodeos are for the adrenaline junkies. It's an athletic sport where we have to have quicker reflexes than a boxer, the fitness o**

a runner and the power to body weight of a gymnast. The whole business of dealing with animals is very rewarding and you have to use your mind in a way that no other sport requires.

Carol Willowbank, QLD

... when you get up each day and fill it with experiences, family and friends. Each day is a bonus.

Joseph
Inala, WA

...freedom

... to have enough food for my stock, peace and goodwill to my friends and neighbors, to be able to work and make enough to live on and have enough spare time to go fishing and pottering about in the outback.

James
Coolah, NSW

… having life long friends who will be there any time you may need to share an experience or want some support. Happiness is also being able to be there for my friends when they need my support. Happiness is laughing with my two sisters, looking at old family photographs and listening to R & B

Daina

Taringa, QLD

... freedom

... knowing our land. My family have been swimming in this billabong for thousands of years.

Catherine

Maningrida, Arnhem Land

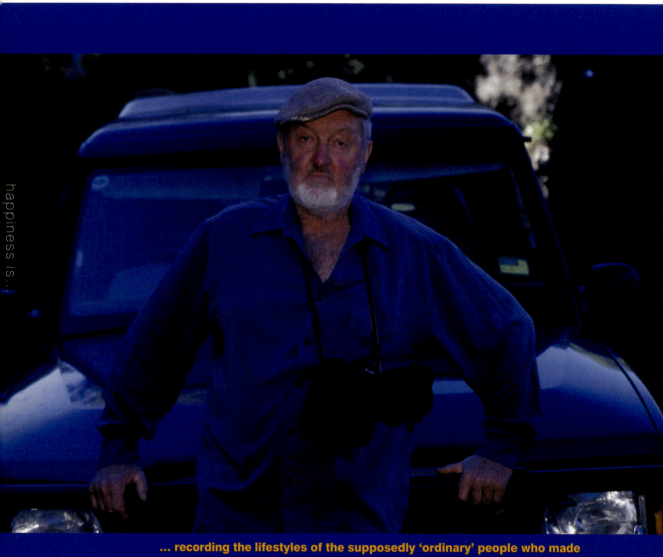

happiness is...

... recording the lifestyles of the supposedly 'ordinary' people who made our nation, whom I call signature Australians. Preferably unposed, candid studies by available light. Making the prints and having them displayed in exhibitions and my forthcoming book.

Jeff
Gerringong, NSW

... closing my eyes at night and having no worries – it is raining, the grass is a foot high, the children are happy and content and I have someone who loves me to cuddle up to.

Margot
Coolah, NSW

happiness is…

…somewhere above this world lives a man in a colourful dream. What better environment to express my colourful nature than in the worlds largest playground.
Te Hau

Woollongong, NSW

... I can't remember my life before football...

Rach
Darlinghurst, NSW

happiness is…

… a gathering of jigglers and danglers who always see the cup as half full, never half empty when taking tea at Noosa Main Beach.

Glennys
Noosaville, QLD

happiness is…

… having fun with family and friends and enjoying every minute of every day. Spending time with my grandparents.

Kassandra
Hazelmere, WA

… spending time with good friends, laughing out loud, sand, sun & ocean. All with a smattering of hard work in between, then relaxing with an ice coldie.

Gus
Leichhardt, NSW

happiness is...

... the WOW factor of every time I step onto my wooden boat which floats on the most beautiful harbour in the world. How lucky am I to jump into our wonderful waters to feel refreshed every time!

Max
Queens Park, NSW

… time spent outdoors, be it at the beach, in a park or anywhere incorporating activities like people watching, and a workout is always a bonus.

Pete
Bondi, NSW

…freedom

invigorating

... posing in an old bath.

Sarah

... having a family and friends who love you and treat you well and just accept who you are and let you enjoy life.

Emma,
Taringa, QLD

happiness is…

… a family, a future, a knowledge of mother nature that allows us to look to supplying the world with food.

John
Condobolin, NSW

… enjoying simple things, sun, water, grass under my feet.

Peter

Miranda, NSW

…freedom

PASSION

I love the word passion and everything it represents. It's full of the power to express yourself. Passion is about having dreams and chasing them with all your heart. Passion to me is an indelible inner strength and determination.

People are often fearful of their passions. They have been programmed into a habitual thinking pattern and as a result live discontented lives. You can't make positive changes until you realise the negative patterns you are perpetuating.

If you don't like what you are doing, change your life and chase your dream now. What are you waiting for? Keep striving, never give up, maintain a positive, passionate outlook. You can take on the world.

Create a new way of living. Change all the rules and believe you can't go wrong — you will find the strength to do whatever it is that you believe in. Take risks. Don't postpone anything for the wrong reasons. If you believe in it enough, you will find a way. Be tenacious and hold on to your dreams until they become a reality.

Create a vision for yourself. Be in love with life. Stay true to yourself and your heart. Use the strength of your passion to become the person you want to be.

Lisa

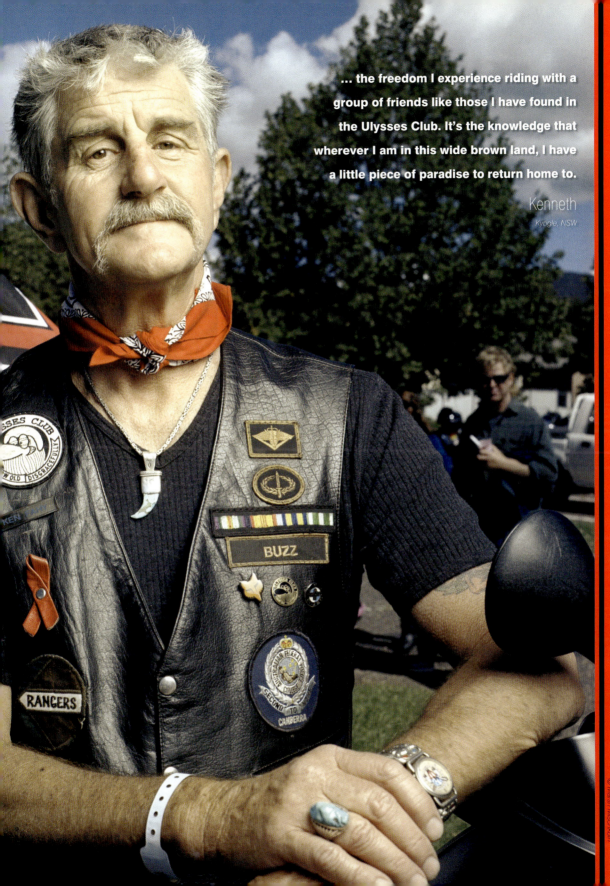

… the freedom I experience riding with a group of friends like those I have found in the Ulysses Club. It's the knowledge that wherever I am in this wide brown land, I have a little piece of paradise to return home to.

Kenneth
Kyogle, NSW

Happiness for me is feeding my friends and family. To be able to cook for people is one of the greatest pleasures for me and a delicious meal is seldom forgotton by hungry mouths at my table. The two hungry mouths I love to feed though are the loves of my life, my cat 'Missy' and my little dog 'Rollo'. Only after dinner time when they both lay flat out in the sun or by the heater does a total state of happiness exist. With full tummies they are at one with each other and the world. I know this to be true as it makes me happy too!

Patrick
Surry Hills, NSW

... when your heart is singing, your mind knows the melody, your body has the rhythm and you're alone playing through life in harmony.

Rebecca
Paddington, NSW

happiness is…

… doing what I love most which is sharing my music with people and making people happy through my music.

Hayley
Lake Munmorah, NSW

… a quality or state of contentment, achievement or delight. Happiness lights up my face with a large smile. This photo is me playing my first gig in a band at a school fete with my new pink fluffy drums. The vibes were great that day as we played the best that we had played!

Marnie
Chain Valley Bay, NSW

…passion

145

performing

… there are many things which make me happy. I love being on tour with my band, performing my music to large crowds, writing new songs, going 4-wheel & motorbike driving in country areas, going camping, horse riding and being with my animals and friends.

Vanessa
VIC

... refreshing days spent at the beach in the warm afternoon sun. You forget about your worries and leave feeling revitalised.

Linda and Mandy
Perigian Beach, QLD

happiness is...

... Aussie Aussie Aussie Oi Oi Oi

Margaret
Wentworth Falls, NSW

… feeling comfortable with yourself and the way in which you interact with others. Happiness is being part of a loving, communicating family. Happiness is earning the respect of others and returning it. Happiness comes from your efforts to be a good person.

Timothy
Rozelle, Sydney

happiness is …

… having good health and my wife and family being close. Enjoying life at its best. I'm so happy to see people in our business being successful with commitment to their job and being rewarded for their efforts.

Bob
Greenfield, SA

… laughter and making people laugh. Enjoying everything and always looking for the best in anything.

Max and Gerry
Gladesville, NSW

happiness is…

© Richard Miller

© Stephanie Allan

...passion

... what I love doing the most – driving and preserving steam locomotives which are at the Bellarine Peninsula Railway in Victoria. I've had a passion for steam trains since I was born! The sight, sound, smell, feel and the skill it takes to drive a steam engine coupled with the adrenalin of firing or driving a 200 tonne steam engine makes me happy.

Tristan
Cliffton Springs, VIC

happiness is …

… doing all things possible to make your life (and that of those around you) stimulating and rewarding – and making sure you see the results.

Seamus
Newtown, NSW

smiling, hugging, kissing

...passion

... having your friends around playing music and talking nonsense.

Mikey
Bondi Junction, NSW

happiness is...

© Andrew Suzuki

... balance of life.

Kenji Ogawa
Putney, NSW

...passion

happiness is...

... being outdoors with my partner Peter and my horses. I love riding and particularly competing, which gives me something to aim for, but I also like just spending time with horses – they are beautiful animals.

Stephanie
Kyneton, VIC

... the small things in life that bring a smile to your face.

Carissa
Marrickville, NSW

...passion

happiness is…

… for me, an eclectic mix … the scent of frangipanis; Sunday afternoon jazz; the blue intensity of summer skies; high heeled boots; the beauty of dry stone walls and wrought iron balustrades; twirling about the dance floor; laughing with my sister; being in my husband's arms; traveling the world…

Meegan
Winthrop, WA

© Adam Poli

... follow your dreams and appreciate what you have because happiness is free. And always remember that all people smile in the same language.

Sean
Pyrmont, NSW

161

happiness is…

Scott's happy stand-in.

… being satisfied with life and making the most of your opportunities. Pursuing your dreams and interests and having great friends and family around you.

Scott
Ballarat, VIC

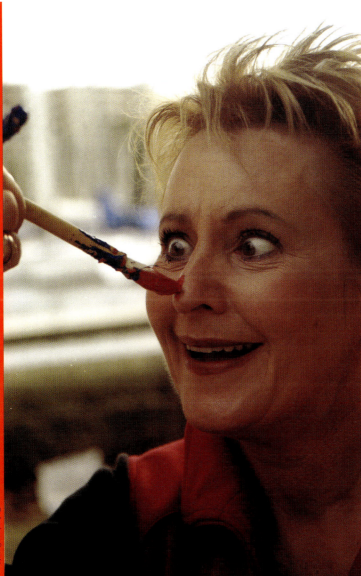

... the company of good friends, some fine food and wine... water lapping against a boat and the buzz of blow flies in the distance. The smell of a fully blown rose, dew between my feet on freshly mown grass, a cuddle of a sleeping baby, giving happiness to someone you love...

...passion

Prue
Rushcutters Bay, NSW

SPIRITUALITY

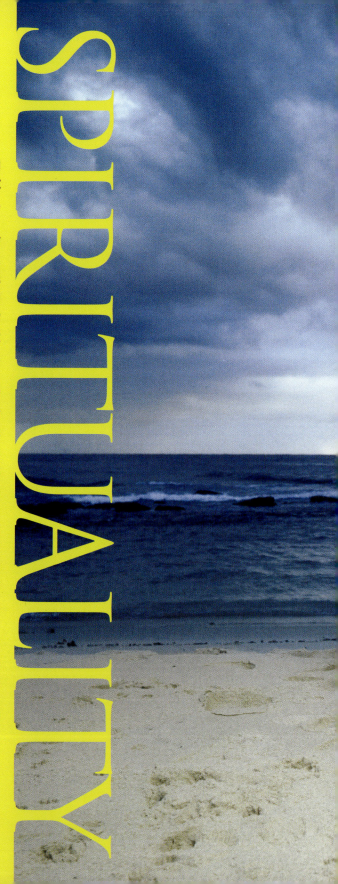

Being at peace with ourselves and being at peace with others is an attitude that moves us to another level of happiness.

To me this is a vital part of spirituality — finding a higher level of inner peace. Spirituality is being at one. It takes us beyond our emotional and intellectual boundaries and shows us that our existence and consciousness connect with something other than ourselves.

It is a sense of basic trust in a higher power and this trust can change our lives. A realisation of spirituality contains within it a surrender to this higher power, and with that comes growth. It's about believing passionately, never doubting.

Spirituality brings a change in our perspective. Our egos often perceive things as being so important, but in the scheme of the universe these things are a mere nanosecond in the blip of existence.

Be centred and at peace. Finding the spiritual dimension to our lives is a voyage of great personal discovery. Take the trip.

Volker and Lisa

… immersion in clean, healthy seas. To be at one with the ocean. The sheer sensual pleasure of ocean swimming, gliding through the surf and sea with human aquatic friends, sunlight or starlight glinting on the surface of the ocean catching swimmers, surfers and snorkellers smiles.

Genevieve
Bronte, NSW

© Martin Mischkulnig

... being married for 43 years and still happy and content. To have a good family and friends. Going to the beach early in the morning to meet with wonderful people. To be 60 years old and still be able to enjoy life.

Malcolm
Lake Cooroibah, QLD

... watching everything the good Lord made.

William
Noosaville, QLD

...spirituality

… that inner feeling of warmth. Friends, love and laughter. Being able to laugh and make others smile. I wish it was a paid profession. Dancing is my passion. I feel free and able to express so much using just movement. Dance makes me happy even if it's only for a three minute song — I forget all my troubles.

Angie
Surry Hills, NSW

…spirituality

rainbows

happiness is....

... being loved by someone who you love just as much. Sitting with your back against a eucalypt with the sun on your face. Diving beneath the waves, letting the ocean wash away your tears.

Nanette
Scarborough, WA

... family, friends, the ocean and beer – all together at a BBQ.

Paul
Scarborough, WA

...spirituality

... good friends, family, chocolates, expensive shoes and a purring cat.

Sammy
Rozelle, NSW

...spirituality

... participating in anything that puts a smile on your face and a warm feeling in your heart. Fishing, fishing, fishing and painting landscapes.

John
Eltham, VIC

happiness is ...

… **as I get older, my life increasingly becomes more complex — what makes me most happy these days are the simple pleasures — time with friends and loved ones, good cooking,**

…spirituality

great surf and strong yoga! Come to think of it, it's always been that way — I guess a return to simplicity is where it's at.

Gabriel
Paddington, NSW

happiness is…

…the radiant love of my family. My grandson, my son and his soul-mate fill me with strength, confidence and happiness. My senses vibrating to the fullness of life. I am happy, I smile, I am positive, I am bold, I am strong. Be true and just be.

Maria
Katoomba, NSW

happiness is…

…bliss

Patricia
Campsie, NSW

Bad hair days gone forever

© Andrew Suzuki

...spirituality

... feeling alive, energy soaring through your body bursting out in a smile. The joy of freedom, flying with friends, dancing with fire, high on life!

Julia
Woolongong, NSW

happiness is...

… connecting with life and Spirit on a daily basis. I sit in a Spiritual Circle which gives me the great privilege of experiencing that connection with teachers or guides whose purpose is to develop us to our highest potential. Through that I have come to know that every person and every living thing on Earth and beyond is connected in Light and Love. Happiness is too small a word for the feeling that comes from experiencing that connection and as a result I strive to see that Light in every contact in my daily life.

Robyn
Summer Hill, NSW

Two days after we did the photo shoot with Arrnott, he rang me and started singing. He said he had been inspired to write a song to reflect the spirit of *Happiness Is...* I feel extremely honoured that the idea of the book touched him enough to do this. I hope you will have the chance to hear it soon.

Thank you Arrnott.

Happiness Is

Arrnott Olssen

© 2004

In the quiet moments
When you're all alone
And the world is still
No ringing telephone
In the busy bustle
Of a crowded street
Basking in the sunlight
Waiting for a treat

I hold a loved one close to me
That's what happiness is
I sing my heart out
Can you hear?

Chorus

There's a joy in the little things in life
There's a peace when your heart has found what's right
It's the moment when you smile and let life flow
It's the wonderment the passionate the joy
That's what happiness is

You can dream your dreams
Follow passions heart
Find a joy that knows
Where the loving starts
It's whatever is
That whatever brings
To fulfil the moment
Where you fly on wings

TOWNS

People represented in *Happiness Is...* are from far and wide.

New South Wales

Armidale 63, 78
Artarmon 117
Balmain 55
Bellevue Hill 16
Berry 17
Bexley 79
Bilgola 10
Bondi 4, 135
Bondi Junction 155
Bomaderry 111
Bronte 164
Burwood 45
Cammeray 68, 97
Caloundra 106
Campsie 178
Castle Cove 36
Cecil Hills 44
Chain Valley Bay 145
Centennial Park 30
Collaroy 58
Condobolin 138
Coolah 121, 125
Como West 59
Crows Nest 77
Darlinghurst 23, 127
Edgecliff 30

Elanora Heights 76
Five Dock 112, 116
Gerringong 124
Gladesville 152
Gordon 41
Harbord 77
Ingleburn 73
Katoomba 176
Kyogle 141
Lake Munmorah 66, 145
Leichhardt 49, 128, 133
Marickville 159
Matraville 104
Miranda 139
Mosman 52, 76
Newtown 69, 154
Paddington 42, 53, 144, 175
Petersham 76
Putney 156
Pyrmont 161
Queens Park 134
Robertson 61, 100
Roseville 54
Rouse Hill 77
Rozelle 64, 150, 173
Rushcutters Bay 163
Summer Hill 180

Surry Hills 142, 143, 168
Sydney 18
Terrigal 75
Tocumwal 25
Wentworth Falls 149
Willoughby 29
Woollahra 57
Woollongong 126, 179
Zetland 70

Nothern Territory
Maningrida, Arnhem Land 83, 103, 110, 123

Queensland
Bundaberg 94
Caloundra 106
Chapel Hill 67
Coolum Beach 96
Cooroy 35, 90
Glenview 89
Lake Cooroibah 166
Maroochydore 8
Maurilyan 48
Moffat Beach 40
Noosaville 130, 167
Paddington 14
Perigian Beach 148
Taringa 122, 136, 137
Twin Waters 98
Willowbank 118
Whitfield 26

South Australia
Greenfield 151

Tasmania
Chain of Lagoons 6
New Town 2

Victoria
Aspendale Gardens 74
Ballarat 162
Brighton 11
Cliffton Springs 153
Eltham 174
Hampton 32
Kialla 12
Kyneton 158
Middle Park 15, 131
Opossum Bay 46
Prahran 62
Toorak 84, 88

Western Australia
Beaconsfield 99
City Beach 92
Dunsborough 38, 47, 56
East Fremantle 172
Hazelmere 132
Iluka 80, 82
Inala 120
Kandinya 95
Leederville 19, 24
Mandurah 1, 72
Maida Vale 114
Mosman Park 93
Nedlands 109
North Perth 50
Queens Park 22
Quindalup 28, 107
Scarborough 86, 170, 171
West Pingelly 102, 108
Winthrop 160
Woodvale 87

I'd love to represent more wonderful people, towns and suburbs in the next edition. If you would like someone you know to appear in a *Happiness Is...* book, please contact me on info@happinessis.com.au

PHOTOGRAPHERS

happiness is...

Thank you to all the wonderful and talented photographers who believed in my dream and helped me realise this vision. Each one of them is incredibly special to me and without them this book would not be a reality. The diversity provided by the different backgrounds of the photographers and subjects helps make this book a true representation of a happy Australia.

It was an absolute pleasure going on the shoots with those of you whom I did. If you, the reader ever needs a talented photographer and like what you see in these pages, please do not hesitate to contact me on *lisa@messengermarketing.com.au*, and with the photographers permission, I would be delighted to pass on their details.

Stephanie Allan, *Geelong, VIC*
… discovered her passion for photography two years ago at only 14 years of age. She is following her interest keenly.

Debbie Amster, *Ashmore Plaza, QLD*
… of Bliss Photography has been creating images professionally for 7 years, while designing them her whole life. Her love of photography began as a small child. Bliss Photography was created to inspire her clients to capture the blissful moments in their lives — romantic weddings, precious little ones, cherubic infants, devoted families. Debbie loves what she does and her enthusiasm and spontaneity is contagious, guaranteed to make you smile! Bliss Photography has recently won two Wedding Industry Awards and are embarking on their first international assignment in July 2004.

Scott Antonio, *Ballarat, VIC*
… has been taking photos for around five years. He has a company called 3G photography. Like any living thing, animals have their own personalities and he gets great enjoyment trying to capture this on film. With his permission, we thought it was a bit of fun to include the highland cow as its so gorgeous.

Anita Arnold, *Surry Hills, NSW*
… is the Executive Personal Assistant to Bradley Trevor Greive. As his logistics expert, Anita has been at Bradley's side for five years, organising every facet of his life… including being on the spot to capture amazing moments like this one. Although not a professional photographer, Anita's study of Architectural Drafting and her background as an Executive PA have enabled her to combine her creative talents and her perfectionist's eye for detail. All attempts were made by BTG to locate other photographers of photos taken of Bradley Trevor Greive.

Dr Magdy Altia, *Burwood, NSW*
… is a 47 year old male medical practitioner born in Egypt. Migrated to Australia in 1984. Photography is his passion. He loves photographing his children as it gives him tremendous joy to see them enjoying themselves.

Penelope Barton, *Newtown, NSW*
… is a commercial photographer who has been fortunate to travel, meeting new people, experiencing diverse cultures and being paid to live her dream.

John Bowie, *Noosaville, QLD*
…is a freelance cartoonist, graphic artist and photographer.

Renee Brazel, *Kangaroo Point, QLD*
… has over five years as a professional photographer specialising in creative portraiture. She has won 10 national and state AIPP awards.

Adrian Brown, *Redfern, NSW*
… is lucky enough to earn a living from advertising photography. Thankfully, he's even luckier to somehow find time to balance his commercial shooting with unique conceptual based work. It is there that he develops projects close to his heart and gets to create intense, vivid and emotional rich images. www.brownbox.com.au

Steve Cavanagh, *Darlinghurst, NSW*
… is currently completing an honours degree in Fine Art at The National Art School, Sydney. He has exhibited in group shows from 2001– 2004. The photographs submitted are from a series of work titled '8 Seconds'. He says the theatre of rodeo is loaded with imagery, both real and fantasy. It takes 100% commitment to survive the speed and danger of this event. He wanted to capture the iconography and nostalgia of the rodeo cowboy.

Ian Clarke, *Canterbury, VIC*
... is 35 years old, married to a beautiful woman named Andi, and lives in Melbourne's outer East. He studied Photography at Phillip Institute at Bundoora in Melbourne, then went on to assist one of Melbourne's leading wedding photographers. He started his own business in 1999, and has photographed over 200 weddings. His favourite pastimes are cycling, renovating his house and playing bass guitar.

Joyce Evans, *Toorak, VIC*
... is well known for her photography of Australia, the outback and it's people, as well as her portraits of notable Australians. She is also a photographic historian and valuer, consultant, curator and lecturer on photography. She has exhibited widely and her work is held in numerous public and private collections. She is a grandmother, a collector and a humanist who enjoys exploring ideas and places. Joyce's warmth, compassion and sense of humour shine through her work.

Bryan Fuller, *Coolah, NSW*
... is an accomplished farmer and grazier in central NSW with a strong interest in photography and cars.

Rachel Fuller, *Darlinghurst, NSW*
... is currently in her first year at Sydney College of the Arts, Rozelle majoring in photography. She has been taking photos for 10 yrs and at present is concentrating on colour work with the emphasis on light and its abstracting qualities.

Natalie Grace, *Cammeray, NSW*
... runs her own business, has a beautiful two year old boy, and loves taking photos (mainly of him).

Mark Green, *Summer Hill, NSW*
... was born in Sydney in 1962. He Joined the NSW police force when he was 19. He served in Sydney, the Snowy Mountains and the Riverina. He is married to a wonderful woman called Robin. He has three teenage boys, a grown up stepdaughter and a grandson. After 23 years service he made a major career switch giving up the police force to become a qualified astrologer. He now enjoys a much more spiritual lifestyle and helping people in a much more loving and gentle way.

Katrina Hawley, *Scarborough, WA*
... is a 32 year old living near the beach in Perth. After working as a PA for years, she finally entered a career in photography so she could put her imagination onto paper and help others do the same.

Mark Hubert, *Camperdown, NSW*
... has 20+ years in management and is embarking on a new profession as a capturer of defining and happy moments. He loves this photo as it shows a sparkling, positive, always happy person, whose presence brightens an otherwise negative and dreary workplace.

Jane Hurley, *Glenview, VIC*
... was a nurse, has travelled extensively and is presently a mum and photography student at Nambour TAFE in Queensland.

Andy James, *Artarmon, NSW*
... is an engineer. These photos are two of the many of Neen taken all over the world in what she calls the "Ta Dah" pose.

Davina Johnson, *Airlie Beach, QLD*
… believes photographs epitomise happiness. She is a second year photography student whose passion is capturing people's emotions on film.

Marion Jonkers, *Woomby, QLD*
… is the proud mother of 22 year old Marayke. Marayke represented Australia at the Paralympic Games in Athens in 2004. She is a world ranked swimmer and Australian champion. Marion is a high school art teacher and is currently in her final year of a photography diploma.

Brett Jones, *Hazelmere, WA*
…loves to take photos of people and whatever he sees as naturally as he can. He would love to publish his own book some day.

Clare Judd, *Beerwah, QLD*
… is studying photography and hoping to continue her passion.

Kristen Little, *Shelly Beach, QLD*
… is a student photographer at CSIT. She is a mother of three children and has been a registered nurse working in aged care for 15 years. She has a special love of people at the beginning of their life and in their golden years.

Steve Lovegrove, *New Town, TAS*
… began in photography in Alice Springs in 1980. In 1983, he established a commercial studio in Darwin and then moved to Hobart in 1988. In over 23 years, his work has featured a range of photographic subjects and styles including advertising, commercial, people, places and self-commissioned projects. His beautiful son was delivered 6 weeks premature by emergency caesarean. The series of photos tells a beautiful and amazing story of hope.

Kylie Lyons, *Narellan, NSW*
… graduated from UTS Nepean with a BA in Design. She began Handprint photography in 1993 and moved into Heritage Studio in 2000.

Robert McMillan, *Woollongong, NSW*
… is a school teacher and a sky diving instructor with 14 years experience. Photography is a personal passion.

Ned Meldrum, *Fitzroy, VIC*
… of Ned Meldrum Photography is known as an international jet setting all star playboy.

Marie Nicole Meunier, *Terrigal, NSW*
… was born in Melbourne, studied visual art and design in Newcastle and is currently running a photography studio in Terrigal on the central coast of NSW

Rose Miletic, *Cecil Hills, NSW*
… of FRESH IMAGES BY ROSE has been photographing weddings and portraits for 14 years and absolutely loves what she does. 'I feel very honoured when people choose me to capture their special moments, weddings especially, there is a sense of pride when people pick up their work and absolutely love what I have created. Some have even cried upon viewing their completed wedding albums and can't thank me enough. I hardly advertise at all these days because most of my work comes from referrals of people that were rapt with what I gave them.' She loves this photo that her husband took.

Richard Miller, *Balmain / Berry, NSW*
… is lucky he loves what he does. Christmas 1900 and something (I'd rather not say the year), my father gave me a Kodak Angfinder Camera and I fell in love with making pictures. My mentors over the years have been Snowdon, David Bailey, Annie Leibovitz and here in Aus, Jeff Carter. The road from the UK around the world many times has filled my life with many warm memories. Rich is the man with friends and in the bank of friendship my cup runneth over. Sophie and Alex, my children, keep me young and a smile on my face. *People* taking pictures of people is my passion.

Martin Mischkulnig, *Bellevue Hill, NSW*
… fell in love with photography after travelling for nearly a decade throughout the world.
www.martinmischkulnig.com

Steve Morris, *Gawler, SA*
…was an interstate transport driver, driving all over this big brown land. Six years ago he decided on a change of career. He is now a freelance photographer / journalist and says its been an exciting journey! Bob Middleton has been around the race circuit as long as Steve can remember and capturing Bob in his moment of victory was something Steve just couldn't miss.

Simon Mossman, *Neutral Bay, NSW*
… is a journalist by trade. He has worked in newspapers, agencies and television and took up photography four years ago.

Evan Papageorgiou, *Bronte, NSW*
… is a freelance photographer and filmmaker. Evan's work is inspired by the innocence and beauty we see in people and our environment. Evan's motivation for his ongoing work in Arnhem Land is aimed at raising positive awareness of indigenous Australians, their beauty as people and their struggles in modern Australia.

Sonia Payes, *Prahran, VIC*
… is a Master Photographer with the AIPP. She has had a number of photography exhibitions and is represented in Melbourne by John Buckley Fine Art. Sonia's photographs have been published in several books on food and travel, as well as photographic magazines. Sonia has won a number of national awards. In addition to photographic art, she has received many commissions for her portraiture.

Cathy Philo,
… is an amateur photographer. She mostly photographs people or places she knows as a way of documenting her life. She's convinced that when she gets old she will reflect on the things she did with her life – not how much money she had (or didn't as the case may be).

Kylee Priddle, *Coolum Beach, QLD*
… is a mother of two studying photography. She loves to travel with her family on weekend camping trips.

Jan Pryor, *Lake Munmorah, NSW*
… is a high school teacher specialising in art and computers. She has been an artist for 20 years and has been concentrating on photography as her main medium for 12 months.

Jim Rolan, *Paddington, NSW*
… was born in New Jersey, USA. He was educated in Vermont and has a BA in American Studies. He learned portrait photography by assisting and shooting in New York City. He has worked as a professional photographer in Sydney for 16 years.

Peter Ryan, *Elsternwick, VIC*
… is a finance broker who used to see only the big picture. Through photography he sees the cameos and likes to capture how he now sees the world.

Petronella Ryan, *Taringa, QLD*
… has been taking black and white photographs for over 40 years. She loves taking photos of people. Her subjects are her family and friends – people who make her happy.

Sarah Ryan, *Taringa, QLD*
… loves making images of multicultural Australia. She is 18 and has been taking photos for eight years.

Liv Stockley, *Bicton, WA*
… says photography has always been a big part of her life and she has been working in the industry for the past 20 years.

Andrew Suzuki, *Surry Hills, NSW*
….has spent the last eight years honing his skills in the film and television industry. After four years as Supervisor of Video Operations at Animal Logic Sydney, working on projects ranging from *Farscape* to the *Matrix*, Andrew decided it was time to start his own company and start fulfilling his own dreams. Behind the lens of a video or photographic camera, he believes in fantastic images and great storytelling.

Angela Taylor, *Cooroy, QLD*
… says 'I am going to be a great photographer. I am in the mid trimester of my life and photography has been my passion for over ten years. I simply love capturing the moment'.

Kathy Tuddenham, *Sanctuary Point, NSW*
… was a photographer in the RAAF. When she left to join her husband she decided to have a go at photographing weddings and loved it.

Pam Verwey, *Hobart, TAS*
…has a degree in fine arts majoring in photography. She was originally a medical scientist but now has a studio mainly photographing weddings and portraits. She is also interested in nudes, landscape architecture, travel and architectural photography.

Damian Webber, *Budgewoi, NSW*
… 'all my shots are like my children – I know every single one of them by name.'

Daniel Whitely, *Roseberry, NSW*
… works as a freelance accountant, loves the surf and movies and dreams of owning a beach house. He took these photos of Aden and Steph because they capture their love of the outdoors and family.

Melissa Wilbraham, *Maroochydore, QLD*
… her passion is photographing people. 'They are so interesting – everyone has a different face. Photography makes me so happy!'

Lisa Wilde, *Sorrento, WA*
… has a diploma in Applied Science (photography). She is a people photographer, specialising in weddings and portraits.

Adrianne Yzerman, *Pingelly, WA*
… is a city girl living on a farm so her passion for photography means her children and anything 'rural' get snapped constantly.

ACKNOWLE

Every single day from having the idea in my head to now, has brought a smile to my face! I thank the universe every day for the momentum this book has gathered, the synchronicity, serendipity and such incredible support from so many people. Thank you to all of you who believed in my vision so strongly and worked so hard to make it happen. Without a doubt, this has been one of the most fun, happy times of my life. So without further ado, thank you to everyone involved in this book but especially...

ACKNOWLEDGMENTS

Russell Jeffery — who guided me through the publishing process, took my vision and turned it into a masterpiece!

Thanks also to Tracey Adams, Kristy and Gary Allen, Kate Bezar, Seamus Burke, Jenni Carbins, The Cobb Girls and especially Sim, Adam Crouch, Hayley Crossing, Amber Daines, Barbara Dobinson, Amanda Earl, Sir John Fuller, Rachel and Claire Fuller, Bradley Trevor Grieve, Roza Bacelas, Katrina Hawley, Robyn Henderson, the staff at Kids Help Line, Volker Krohn, Angus McConnel, Richard Miller, Ingrid Mogeson, Carmel Molloy, Arrnott Olssen, Stephanie Ridgeway, Angie Ross, Dr Tim Sharp PHD, Andrew Suzuki, Craig Tunnell, and Rhonda Whitton.

Thanks also to everyone who has inspired me and all the amazing and talented photographers and people who are included in this book.

Thank you to JVC and Polaroid for support with prizes for consumer and trade promotions. Thank you to Pierre Winter and Cromwell's; Dean Brunne and Bondi Beer Company; and Jones the Grocer for such enormous support with the launch.

Happiness Is... **has grown a life and momentum of its own. There are so many people who have supported it and I'm sure there will be many more people to thank when it next goes to print.**

happiness is...

... support from close friends